28 SELECTED DUETS

FOR TWO SAXOPHONES (OR OBOES)

(Intermediate – Advanced)

Compiled and Edited by

JAY ARNOLD

These duets have been compiled from the works of masters of composition who have given special significance to the importance of the Clarinet in the world of music.

They are excellent preparatory material for the advanced stages. Each player should diligently practice his part in solo form before associating the performance with the other part.

CONTENTS

ASHLEY
PUBLICATIONS
Distributed by
Hal Leonard

TEN DUETS

J. SELLNER

Allegro non troppo

Allegro vivace

2

Andante con moto

3

Andante sostenuto

6

Allegro vivace

7

Allegro moderato

Adagio con espressione

EIGHTEEN DUETS
From Opus 11

J. H. LUFT

Moderato

Allegretto

3

Andante sostenuto

Allegro con spirito

Tempo I

Allegretto

7

58

Scherzando

8

Moderato

Moderato

11

Allegro meno vivace

Allegro vivace

13

Moderato

15

Andante con moto

Moderato assai

Un poco meno lento

Fine

D.C. al Fine